Visions
Adrift In A Sea Of Echoes

Gary Manz

Published by

SHAMBHABI
The Third Eye Imprint

Published by: Prabir Roy at **Shambhabi – The Third Eye Imprint**, A-10/1, Amarabati, Sodepur, Kolkata 700110, India.

1st edition (USA): November, 2015

Global Distributor: Shambhabi – The Third Eye Imprint

Edited by: Don Martin (Tucson, Arizona)

Cover design: Partha Pratim Das

ISBN-13: 978-93-85783-61-6 [Paperback]

Price: USD 7.99 only

Visions is the window to the mind of Gary Manz, the poet! As I began to read, he did not just let me peer in. Rather, at times, the poem was laced with such intense emotion that it literally clenched me with two hands and pulled me right in. There I now stood in his world. Living what he had lived that day. When reading Gary's work, he gives his readers a strong psychological understanding of human emotion.

There are over 78 different types of poetry ranging from concrete and didactic, to light verse, sonnet, and prose poems. Where does Gary's work fit in all of that? Maybe a place all its own. A hybrid of sorts?

If you read *Visions*, it will be worth every moment you spent on the book. You are reading a book written by a man who has shifted gears his entire life. He has endured the very heights of frustration from all that the world has tossed his way. Suffered massive trauma and survived. He has suffered from cancer, which almost took his life and … survived. He has lived the wild adventures of life's highway. He has also experienced the highest peaks of happiness and joy with his family and friends. And the best part of it all? He has invited you into his life, to share it.

So get in, place your hands on the wheel, and shift gears with him. If you listen carefully, you can hear all 18 wheels slashing the asphalt with a vengeance. Enjoy the ride, as you run adrift in the sea of echoes. I certainly did.

Brian Carlson
Green Bay Wisconsin
October 2015

[Brian Carlson is a renowned writer and author. His works include *Life Through A Windshield*, and children's books including *So Long, Old Hat*, while *Dad, Me, and the 'OL 66' Pete* has been scheduled for release in November 2015. He and his wife Jennifer Ann, are the founders of the charitable foundation drive4freedom.com, dedicated to enhancing and improving the lives of professional truck drivers, their families and friends they love.]

DEDICATION AND ACKNOWLEDGEMENTS

Ordinarily, these are two separate listings but I truly don't know how to separate them, so therefore I'll combine them.

I dedicate this book foremost, to YOU, the reader. I don't care if you purchased it new off of Amazon, bought it for 25 cents at a garage sale, or if it was given to you by a friend or even in a book giveaway. The simple fact is ... if you get any enjoyment, satisfaction, or personal fulfillment out of it ... *this is dedicated to you.*

As far as acknowledgements, they are too numerous to name individually. My grandparents, Emil and Dorothy Manz, would have to be foremost for always supporting me in all of my endeavors. I'd especially like to thank my grandpa for never failing to subscribe to *Readers Digest* and testing me on the vocabulary section every month!

Special thanks also goes to my loving wife who has never failed to be a beacon of faith to guide my path, and numerous friends both old and new along with family members who encouraged me to pursue this path rather than pitching my poetry into the recycle bin as I always had done before. This book wouldn't exist without all of your support.

And without the faith of my friends Kiriti Sengupta and Don Martin, all of these words would truly be ... dust in the wind.

INTRODUCTION

People underestimate the power of words
They can build an empire for the ambitious
They can even crush the dreams of a child

Words

I believe that every person's actions, thoughts, and decisions are guided by the images and echoes of their past.

Echoes of what we've learned and experienced through life. From our parents, grandparents, friends and loved ones.

But also from those we hate, despise, and condemn.

The echoes and images of that past weave together to combine and form the tapestry of who we are.

Unfortunately for me, they often turn into a *sea* of echoes which are often the cause of my insomnia of which I so often write about. I truly hope you enjoy this book and its brief glimpse into my heart and soul.

Gary Manz
October, 2015
Crivitz, Wisconsin

Midnight Echoes

I sit to think
My mind perplexed

My thoughts unfocused
It has me vexed

No words of wisdom
Inspiration to guide

Nothing but silence
It has me beguiled

But I know that in a moment
When I try to sleep

A thousand images
In my mind will creep

From the images of the past
To the thoughts of the morrow

From my joyous days
To my heartaches and sorrows

There is no 'pause' button to silence my head
Just a chorus of voices
To which I am led

Chapter 1

A MOTHER'S LOVE

I was raised by my grandparents after my mother abandoned me to them. She had divorced my father who was serving in the Vietnam War at the time and was incapable of raising me. Something which is all too familiar to too many people, I trust.

Around 12 years ago, I discovered that I had a sister living in Iowa which is where my mother had settled after she left me. She had basically 'sold' my sister to her adoptive parents, giving her up immediately after birth while still at the hospital.

Around five years ago, I discovered that my mother had given birth to another sister out west after changing her identity and after I contacted my new sister, she told me that I also had a brother who had drowned many years ago. Also due to my birth mother's neglect.

As far as my new sister, who had been 'raised' by mother, I discovered that she had a horribly traumatic life which has left her emotionally scarred to this day.

I've only written a single poem about my birth mother and that's probably all I ever will. I've come to the conclusion that she was mentally ill; however, that doesn't change the lives she altered and/or destroyed.

I should also note too that I have two lovely sisters by my father after he returned from the war and remarried. I've

known them since their birth and although we've never been
particularly close, I love them very much.

Mother, Other

One child laughs
One child sighs
One remains silent
While another cries

And the one who bore them all will never know

The first was a boy
Healthy and strong
But in a year you left
That doesn't seem long

Would the rest ever know?

And then a girl
Given up at birth
But raised with love
By the salt of the earth

Without you, they will thrive and grow

Then another girl
But much to my disdain
You kept this one
You should be ashamed

The results will later show

Lastly, another boy
Whose light soon dims

Lost as a child
A consequence of your sins?

Ashes to ashes, and the wind blows

This is what has been reaped
From the seeds you had sewn
Lives in disarray, one lost
Due to a mother ... unknown

A lifetime of deceit and lies
You were a pro

The most powerful demon you will ever face is hindsight.
And its name is...
I wish I would have...

Chapter 2
UN(SCHOOL)ED

I was never a fan of the public school system. Today, there are many public service messages in America about "bullying." What amuses me is when I see a former bully of mine who now has children of his or her own, posting anti-bullying messages on his or her Facebook page.

Perhaps they have an even worse memory than I do. Or perhaps they still have an egocentric "I am more important to the world" attitude. I don't know. Then again, I suppose I could give benefit to the doubt that they've simply matured with age which is probably the case. The expression "kids can be cruel" does exist for a reason, after all.

I've lost over 50% of my memory due to brain surgery and other head injuries. But I still remember enough to know how much I hated going to school.

I had no self-confidence or self-worth until my latter teen years. I've paid the price for that.

All I'm saying is that if you see, or your child talks about, a quiet kid who doesn't seem to fit in ... encourage him/her to befriend them. Or better yet, offer your own friendship. Odds are that *you* will be the better by far for it ... as will they.

Table For One

Alone

So alone

Always so alone

But why always alone?

Was it my choice alone?

You never cared, I sat alone

Alone while the others laughed and played

Alone with my thoughts ... tortured

Alone, but crying within

Alone, awareness denied

Alone ... always

Alone

An Echo's Scream

I hear the words but cannot speak

My mind betrays the thoughts I seek
Emotion hidden deep inside
It steals away. It runs. It hides.

A smile masks away the frown
The saddened soul, replaced by clown
No tears of laughter, tears of joy
Just frightened thoughts, of a frightened boy

The years have passed, but still ... within
Like the hurt and anger ... worn with a grin
The rest of the world will never know
For these things I speak of, I seldom show

I am a man of constant sorrow
Hoping the past will change
With the advance of the morrow
The day approaches when I'm laid to rest
I fear that day might be my best

Memories

I remember here

I remember now

I remember fear

I remember how

To you, it was jocularity

I find no hilarity

And nothing further was said

For we'll all soon be dead

Misspent Youth

Thrust into an alien world
A newborn cries
Innocent tears of youth

Growth and discovery
Exploring good and evil
Mastering neither
He sheds the tears of the uncouth

As his innocence fades
With passing age
He forges his steely armor
And sharpens his blades
His tears slowly turn to rust

Now, alone in his room
Filled with passionless gloom
Emotionally drained
Well aware of his doom
His soul, a lifeless desert
Wiping away his tears of dust

The Reaper grins

Final Bow

It hung from a string

This despicable thing
Strung from the corners of his mind
To his carnivorous soul

To be beaten and prodded
Like some ghoulish piñata
To survive the anguish...
That was the goal

He barely felt the blows from antagonists
For he was a protagonist
Author and star of his own play
He knew it was what he could expect

But he could feel the sting
From every swing
Of a so called friend, or so he had thought
But he hid the pain and met it with jest

The most horrific stains
Caused by the most hideous pains
Were from those that he knew as his loved ones
He had never written it into his part

Of hope and joy, it has left him bereft
Nearly time to exit 'stage left'
After one final close-up
Of his torn and shattered heart

Funny thing about feelings that I've observed over my time on this marble.

Those who have the least amount of feelings get them hurt the least. I've also noticed that those same people tend to walk around in a zombie state with a joyless expression on their faces and spread ... well ... *nothing* to those whom they meet.

Conversely, those with the most feelings often get them hurt. Sometimes daily, but in most cases at least monthly, or certainly numerous times per year.

Those are also the same people that you see smiling, laughing, and playing. They write the songs that you hear and sing along to. The books you read. The humor that makes you laugh.

They ignite and excite the passion and fire in your heart and soul and make the world around you worth living in.

Anytime you allow your feelings to show you take the chance of having them hurt, or even worse, simply ignored.

But that's the price one has to pay for truly being alive.

The trick to being happy within is not the ability to suppress one's feelings. It's the ability to embrace them and move forward. They are a part of you. No amount of willpower will ever change that. The only question in the end is ... are you going to own them? Or are they going to own you?

Chapter 3

MY LOVE ... MY LIFE ... MY WIFE

The day I met my wife made my life complete. She is everything that I've always lacked. Composure, confidence, love, an appreciation of *being*!

It's probably safe to assume that I would most likely not be alive today were it not for her. I'd likely be dead of an overdose or stupidity or ... well *perhaps* they're one and the same. Just another victim of self-abuse and hatred.

I see and think of her everywhere I go. In everything I do. I have many regrets in life but my biggest regret is that I'll never be able to return to her what she has given me.

For you Sharon, my love of 27 years ... and counting.

Gazing At The Window

Such complexity contained within simplicity.

I stare into her eyes with the wonder of an innocent child
staring into a wishing well with coin in hand.

Looking closer, I know why they're so hard for me to
define.
Not blue, green, hazel ... and yet ... all of them and so much
more.
As a glint of sunlight bathes across them, I can see all the
colors of the spectrum.
Emerald green, royal blue, but what's most striking are the
shining flecks of gold.

A fitting portal to her heart.
Her soul.
And my incredible fortune in having her grace my
otherwise colorless life.

Slowly, her eyelids begin to flutter and she's gently lulled to
sleep.

In my mind.

Regrets

I see a face, and think of you

Regrets?

I've had a few

A perfect place

A perfect time

This sort of thing is never mine

Regrets?

I've had a few

And most of them

Look just like you

Never Less, Never More

As I lay here weak and weary

With my eyes and thoughts so bleary

I think of Sharon, my life, my love, my "Lenore"

But whereas Edgar Allen Poe was napping

I lay here, my thoughts are rapping

Tap, tap, tapping until my head is sore

How lucky can one man be?

To have met a godsend such as she

She fills my life right down to my inner core

And although the years keep ticking

In my heart and soul, she's sticking

I could ask or want for nothing more

This is my wish for you

To find someone just as true

As my dream, my desire, my Sharon, my "Lenore"

And as for Edgar Allen Poe

It's just too bad he'd never know

There's only one true love in life

And for me, it is my wife

I'll quote the raven now

"Never more"

Spooner's Moon, Swooner's Tune

The stars and the moon

Carry a tune
And all those who hear it
Begin to swoon

A song through the ages
Oft heralded by sages
Who pen it in verse
And fill up their pages

It croons *amoré*
To a young girl and boy

A gentle hand to hold
As we begin to grow old

But there are those who won't hear
They turn a deaf ear
Wandering alone through life
Year after year

Yet, all this can change
Let them sing out your name
Open your heart
And tend passion's flame

One can never truly know what lies in the heart of another
man's soul. But through poetry, one can define the nature of
that soul.

Chapter 4

MY COUNTRY ... *"TIS OF THEE"*

Much the same as with most people, I've had a lot of jobs over the years.

I've worn a name tag on my shirt in the service industries. I've walked around in steel-toed boots in factories and power plants. I've worn a suit and tie as an insurance and annuity representative. I've disappointed my father because I didn't pursue a career in psychology after graduating college.

But to me, the most important thing in the far too short time we have on the planet, is to be happy in what you do. And what makes me happy is to drive!

It began with my first car. A '73 Olds Cutlass Supreme with Crager rims, 350 Rocket V-8 4-bolt main engine, a super-shifter racing transmission, Redline tires, and air shocks ... or so I recall! And proudest to me is that I bought it with money I'd been saving since I was 12 years old.

For the last 21 years, I've been a truck driver. I have no boss looking over my shoulder. I set my own schedule. I've seen more sunrises, sunsets, and shooting stars than most people will see in a lifetime, assuming that they live to be 500 years old.

More importantly though, is that I take the time across my travels to actually stop and *explore*. Life is too short, in my humble opinion, to spend it living in a cubicle by day and a box called home by night.

I've seen the typical tourist attractions like the Grand Canyon, Niagara Falls, etc. But what impresses me most are the 'out of the way' things.

The 40-foot-tall statue of the Jolly Green Giant in Blue Earth, Minnesota. The giant meteor crater in Arizona. The huge bat cave in New Mexico. And most of all, the landscape itself.

My point is ... don't just *live*. LIVE!

Refuel ... Slowly

I drove two million miles as of this year

Something of a *milestone*

They must have all been in circles
Since they always brought me home

It started with a single mile
Soon followed by ten more
It started with a single smile
Which, upon my face, I wore

And quickly it was a hundred, then a thousand, then 10k
Around the country I did roam
But much to my dismay

A hundred thousand miles passed
But I'd seen nothing at all
Just a blur of trees ... rocks ... white lines and cars
From winter through the fall

Then I decided to smell the roses

Take time to stop and look
To shut down when I'm in someplace new
Get my nose out of my book

Since then, I've explored meteor craters
Bat caves ... canyons ... great falls
From the Jolly Green Giant in Minnesota
To New Orleans Mardi Gras

I've tried to see it all

After a million miles
There was so much left to do
I decided to keep on driving
And so, I'm now at two

Thousands of sunrises to the east
And sunsets to the west
Rainbows ... shooting stars ... more than most see in a
lifetime
It's impossible to choose which one was best

Life's too short to stay in cubicles
Or stare at factory walls
To spend years in a job you tolerate
Just for a weekend or short vacation, to recover from it all

So take time off
Get out ... see ... feel
Set your mind and soul free

These are the things I'll concentrate on
As I drive toward million three

Clueless Companions

As the masses snuggle contently in their beds
The sky erupts with fiery passion

It's time for Mother Nature to party

While the tendrils of electric light stretch their tentacles
out to touch the horizon
The trees begin to dance and sway to the chorus which
surrounds them

The clouds weep with joy as they swim through the
darkness

And when Morpheus finally releases his tender grip
The day walkers will only know that it must have rained
last night

Life and nature will forage on

To Err Is ... Human

Powder blue sky
Charged with energy
Resilient resolution
Furnished ... furnaced...
Lemon yellow sun

Emerald fields
A sea of green
Teamed with life
Both noticed, and unseen
Flowered ... scoured...
Exploited by all

Aquamarine scene
Vast oceanic depth
Strangest of all
A world of its own
Creatures ... features...
Monsters of the deep

Instruction ... seduction
Infraction ... reaction
Mankind ... destruction

The Playful Mind

It just hangs there
Silent
Unmoving
As if daring me to come play
To touch it
Become part of its world
The little boy within me heeds its call

Hard to define at this distance
Like a cat curled up sleeping
With just a trace of the powder blue carpet it lays on
Shining through the center
Or perhaps a Caribbean atoll
Encompassed in a billowy early morning mist

I call out to it with my mind
Beckoning for an answer
Some explanation
I imagine hearing hushed whispers from its friends
Snickering with glee at my confusion

But all I truly hear is the gentle breeze
The other clouds know its name
They remain stoically silent
As they begin to sculpt their next enigma

A Respective Perspective

As I look at the countryside around me
It never ceases to astound me

The wondrous beauty that surrounds me

If we only would stop to look

The old year has finally passed

A perfect time to stop for a breath at last

To take stock of the things we've amassed

Relax ... rewind ... *to play* ... read a book

But most will only stare straight ahead

Some through rose colored glasses, others with dread

Listening mostly, to the voices in their head

Venturing little, from the safety of their nook

Black And Blue

It crept upon me like a whisper

Fall's dark and bitter sister
Or perhaps I feel it more with passing age

The trees around me creak and moan
Their branches snap like brittle bones
Another war on winter's fury has been waged

But the storm will run its course
The arctic winds will lose their force
The steel grey sky will slowly turn to brilliant blue

And once again in all its splendor
The sun compels us to remember
That even the darkest days will pass
They always do

I, Grasshopper

From moment to moment
Day to day
I shuffle and trifle on

Paying no heed
To the reaper's steed
Whose stride is steady and strong

Why live for the morrow?
A constant sorrow
A nightcap for today's abyss

Live for the fraction
The shortest reaction
The cheapest second of bliss

No need to fret
About things I won't get
Why worry about the material?

I long for 'today'
For the 'come what may'

For the here
For the now

The ethereal

One cannot deny the true nature of oneself. In a world where stupidity reigns, it will be the wise who are the most ignorant.

Chapter 6

GOD, IMPENDING DOOM, AND STUFF LIKE THAT

In the last 10 years, I've had my neck broken twice in eight places. I have the breast bone of a cadaver holding my head in place with titanium screws. I've had a major heart attack with 100% blockage and it was well over one hour until I made it to a hospital. I've had emergency brain surgery which led to a huge loss of memory (as well as delusions which would make an awesome story in their own right).

I've died (loss of heartbeat and respiration) seven times and am still here to tell you about it.

I've had many people tell me that obviously God has kept me here for a reason.

Maybe.

Perhaps to serve as an example of how *not* to live your life. In any case, it has served to remind me of how fragile life is. How short. How sweet. It also keeps me in constant pain which adds to my insomnia and general distress. As I've advised earlier, don't simply live ... LIVE!

I've been asked if I ever saw 'the light' during one of my many deaths. No. There was only one unexplained thing that ever happened. During my heart surgery in New Mexico, I was awake and listening as the surgeons were calling out my vital signs. The surgeon above me, near my head, counted down until he finally said, "No pulse, no heartbeat. We're losing him." I couldn't believe what I was hearing.

So right then, I opened my eyes and looked at him and said, "You haven't lost me," and closed my eyes. That was the last thing I remembered until I woke up in the recovery room.

When I woke up, the surgeon was sitting next to me. After the usual questions, "Do you know where you are? What day is it?" etc. he asked if I knew who he was. I told him I did and that he was my surgeon. He asked if I remembered telling him he hadn't lost me. I told him I did. That's when he told me that it should have been impossible for me to have said a single word. He said I'd been drugged and should have been unconscious and even if I wasn't, the respirator and the fact that all life signs had vanished should have made it impossible for me to open my eyes and talk. He was very disturbed. He also seemed a bit disappointed when he asked if I had seen any light or tunnel or past family etc., and I replied that I hadn't.

And I have nothing more to add to the subject. I believe in God. Perhaps not the same way that you do but it seems to me that *how* you believe in God isn't quite as important as *that* you believe. The universe is too perfect and orderly to have been some sort of freakish coincidence.

Natural Design

I am the wind
Fierce and strong
Yet gentle and soothing
When I'm happy in song
My spirit is free
Devoid of sin
For I am the wind

I am the rain
You'll need me to grow
To feed your body
Replenish your soul
I flood your world when I'm angered
But I've no need to explain
For I am the rain

I am the sun
To make your world whole
To brighten your days
And fire your soul
I may sometimes burn you
But I make days such fun
For I am the sun

I gave you the wind, rain, sun, and much more
To make your heart sing
And your spirit soar
All these gifts are for you
To use or abuse
For I am God

Cycle Of Life

I am born of recycled life

Atoms forever, twisting and spinning, form my flesh
Raw, undefined energies coalesce to form my soul
I am, therefore I think

Gaining knowledge and strength daily, I grow
I am the flame
Burning so brightly that I can darken days, and enlighten
nights
I am the power of youth

Gradually the energy is tamed
The flame is tempered
I am the ember
Glowing to provide heat and spark to those who follow
behind

Soon enough, the ember grows dim
I cool and fade, and all that I was, becomes a whisper of a
memory
At last, I become nothing more than ashes, to be scattered
across the ages
I am returned to the recycle bin whence I once sprang

I am born of recycled life
To be continued...

Powder Blue To Soulless Black

He looks toward the heavens
No expression on his face
Marveling at the world's symmetry
Of its beauty
And its infinite grace

Breathing in a perfect day
His thoughts continued to roam
At the majesty that's surrounding him
This blue marble
He calls home

He knows inside
There's no way to hide
A structured balance such as this
It makes him sad, the opinions some have
That God simply doesn't exist

Perhaps not in man's written word
It was, after all, penned by mortals
He's curious how one can peer into the night sky
And still have a blind eye
After viewing all God's portals

A Cardinal's Crown

He searches forth

From dawn to dusk
If for nothing but a morsel
Crimson head tall and proud
Surveying his surroundings

He knows not of mankind's world
It's not in his vernacular
He knows not of the beauty he possesses
No idea of his 'spectacular'

He searches only for a worm
Or bug, or something similar
A thing to make his day complete
Something to fill the void

To most who might view him, he's just a bird
Something they might consider somewhat absurd
But to me, there's an intrinsic beauty
A cardinal's crown
A self-imposed duty

To remind us all, we're not alone
This big blue planet is not our own
We're all in it here together
Whether skin, fur, hair, or...
Feather

Children Of Sol

Growing and thriving in skies of blue
Absorbing the summer warmth

Following its guide and God

Day after day it stretches towards the heavens

Blissful in its own existence

Ignorant of anything other than its deity

Soon God grows impatient

Spending ever less time with its child

Days grow short and nights grow cold

As the shrill autumn wind approaches

The sunflower hangs its head

And weeps

A Journey Home

No more teardrops in my eyes

Wiped away

Returning to their brothers in the skies
Swept along by the winds of fortune
Drawn higher and higher
By the warmth of the sun's fire
Farther and farther away
From their cradle, spawned by gloom

Dancing, spinning, building flair
Guided by starlight
As they wander through the night air
Making a voyage around the world
Growing colder, they despair
Their cloud of comfort feels the pain
Pushes them out
They fall as rain

But I view the cloud through the eyes of a little boy
It simply weeps with joy
At being able to return my tears
To be reborn year after year
Once again
Returned home

Checkmate

I lie upon the waxen board
Face flaxen, nearing death
Overcome by the stench of the thronging horde
I draw in my final breath

Ruled through life by kings and queens
Always following orders
Striving for will, yet lacking the means
A rook at every border

In days of old, when knights were bold
I might have been a soothsayer
But in a world of bought and sold, with no wealth to hold
Even the bishops offer no prayer

I'll just be replaced on the board, by a new generation of
hordes
To be enslaved working from dusk to dawn
As the new royals absorb, all that they can afford
Such is the life ... *and death* ... of a pawn

A Bee's Eye View

How little we're involved in the universe that surrounds us

As we stand on our marble and gaze toward the sky

As though staring through the eye of a needle at a world that's beyond us

Shapes forever shifting ... distorted...

A landscape half gone

We work and we toil, to grow and to thrive

Thus, must seem *our* world

To a bee in its hive

It may be true that all the world's a stage and we are merely players. But I think that the casting director might have been high at the time.

Chapter 7

INSOMNIOMNIOMNIA

I find it odd that this might be the shortest intro in the book, to the greatest demon I face. Those familiar with long-term insomnia will relate.

When it hits, I am truly half alive, but mostly dead.

When Last I Practice

Time again for the spider's ball
Dancing in silence between the walls
Clouding thoughts with silken webs
Spinning a luxurious den of dread

Behind my eyes they spread their fears
Whispering madness in my ears
Ticks, tocks, creaks, moans
My mind, no longer thought's happy home

How can I stop this cavalcade?
Where can I find cerebral Raid?
I beg for silence, plead for peace
But still they dance, they just won't cease

I convince myself that I'll win this time
Find heavenly slumber, sleep divine
But their ball grows in number, this I perceive
Oh what a tangled web I weave

Twilight Parade

Fear of darkness

Fear of light
Lurking in the dim twilight
Always searching for the chance to cause derision

Learn their secrets
Know their names
Watch them as they play their games
Beware the role they play in your decisions

They'll cause you strife
They'll give you hell
Ask the insane, they know them well
Left alone, they'll gnaw away your spirit

Greed, jealousy, paranoia, indecision
These are just to name a few
But there are more, this much is true
They're calling out your name, you just don't hear it

The Quick And The Dead

They lay together

The quick and the dead
And so shall it always be

Writhing in anguish
From what the voices have said
And from the images they barely see

They refuse to sleep or rest at night
Always growing in number

Quarreling, whispering, babbling on
Denying a moment's slumber

In time they'll fade away to dust
Their steely words will turn to rust

But until that day
Within my head
Plays the chorus
Of the quick and the dead

And I shall feel no peace at night

Alone In The Dark

Alone in the dark
The air is still

I wish my mind were so

Drifting along

A piece of flotsam

To what end, I do not know

Cursing the darkness

Yet craving it's peace

Waiting for the wind of fortune to blow

An Army Of None

Relentless
Repent-less
Like a million-man army marching across the tongue of my
mind in their stockinged feet

Never halting
Always faulting
Pointing out every flaw that I've ever missed since my first
consciousness

An errant sound
A forgotten frown
An itch too deep to scratch yet too powerful to ignore

Never stopping for rest
Always doing their best
To seek out and destroy any chance of comfort or joy in the
respite I wish to enjoy

They constantly grow in number
Wishing to annihilate my slumber
Forcing me to fight back with a barrage of cursed verse
when all I truly seek is

Peace...

Of mind

A senior poet can be one who has never shared his thoughts
with others. A senior scholar can be one who never attended
school. And a senior wise man, can be one who recognizes
both.

Chapter 8

THE DIVINE MIND

Poetry is an exploration of what is around the mind's eye. In a way, it's the same as a spelunker who awaits the discovery around the next tunnel of the cave he explores. The only boundaries are ... imagination. Nothing is too absurd ... or forbidden.

I developed an interest in poetry while I was still a child in grade school. Edgar Allen Poe was, and still is, my favorite poet of all time. I love most the way good poetry paints a picture in your mind as well as telling a story.

Although I've been writing poetry for 40 years or so, it was only just over a year ago that I began saving or sharing them. Prior to that, I would write one, keep it for a week or two and read it, then throw it away. I can't even fathom the hundreds or thousands of them that were sent to the recycle bin. I never really knew there was an audience for poetry or that anyone would ever even like what I wrote. It was at the urging of a few family members and Facebook friends that I should keep and share my thoughts and I hope you're not disappointed in them.

Dream Weaver

Viewing life through kaleidoscope lenses
Searching for undiscovered secrets

Exploring a soul, not wholly their own

Unable to tame it

To contain it

They explode into verse

The music of the muse

Misunderstood by many

Often ignored by others

With pen in hand

And dreams in tow

Marches on...

The poet

Animosity Within

As I fare my way across a sea of candor

Searching for the distant shore of my morrows

I struggle to meet my toll

The price? Honesty
The toll? My soul

An altogether unpleasant exchange between that which
I am
And what I wish to be

Drifting wayward
Seeking direction

Hoping the expanse of time and space will allow me to use
what few abilities I possess
For course corrections

I fear it is too late
All for naught

For how can one truly change the nature of a beast within?

To tame a lifetime of internal rage ... and fear

These things are better left caged inside then allowed to
rule

And control destiny

And so I'll drift

Flotsam on this sea of growing despair

Deserted In Good Company

Breathing words
I exhale my thoughts
Which tickles my cerebrum
Random notions
In my mind
Defying rhyme or reason

Morning breaks
With fiery skies
Igniting hidden passion
But the words won't focus
Coalesce
They've run into a bastion

For one like me
There's no greater pain
An amputated poet
But it afflicts the finest
I'm not an island
And it comforts me to know it

Ashes To Ashes

I hold in my hand, the ashes of a broken dream
Once, in my youth, it was merely a seedling
Budding as a spring growth
Seeking only to be nourished in order to blossom
For all the world to marvel in its grandeur
Its flame burned with intensity
Passion
Lighting all that surrounded it
Lack of nourishment for my soul spelled its demise
What was once a glimmer of hopefulness for happiness
Became a quest for self-destruction
A flower grows in a busy field of thistles
Soon it's crowded by the noisy weeds that surround it
Water fails to reach its roots
And it's much larger world chokes the sun from its leaves
The result is inescapable
It simply gives up after much struggle and allows itself to
die
How different are we as supposedly evolved creatures?
I once met happiness
Touched and caressed it and
For a brief shining moment
Allowed myself to fan the embers of my dream
Duty, honor, and obligation presided
And again, the dream was left to smolder into ashes
I find myself searching the horizon for some sign of a
breeze
Like a willow wisp in the desert struggling to survive
A lonely flower in a stagnant field
An empty soul in a darkened room
I seek a gentle wind to scatter the ashes of all that I am
Into all that I dreamed I could be
I wish for my hand to be empty

Defeat is not the true failure

To not have tried.
That is the true failure

Chapter 9

GLASS COLORED ROSES

I was raised by my grandparents and although it was my grandfather who taught me what it was to be a man and he was generally an optimist, I suppose my outlook on life is much more similar to my grandmother who was often quite a pessimist and could always find the dark side of any occasion ... *or so grandpa said anyway!*

So rather than looking through rose colored glasses at the world, as many do, I tend to look at the world as a thorn rather than a rose. Always a threat to cut into you like a dagger when you pay attention least. But even so, I try to retain hope and am always joyful to find the roses in life scattered between the thorns.

I also try to meet life with as much humor as I can muster. My sense of humor tends to be rather quirky though. An example of that is the fact that this book skipped from chapter 4 to chapter 6 with no chapter 5. Most probably wouldn't notice something like that but it would, and *has*, driven me insane when I run across something like that myself so it cracks me up to think there may be someone else out there with that same pet peeve! I'm fairly certain that is directly due to my aunts and uncles who were, and are, so full of life and laughter. I hope you will agree as you read this final chapter.

Detoxymoron

Do whatever makes you happy
Rum and coke won't leave you crappy

Imbibe as much as you may like

Never give in to all the hype

Know that you're the one who's right

Right will *always* beat their might

Even when they say you're stewed

Suck down another shot or two!

Pathetic, how jealous they are

Once they know you're at a bar

Need a way to get there quicker?

Skip the water and drink it thicker!

Instead of quitting once you fall down

Buy yourself another round!

Laugh at those who laugh at you

You know they want to be just like you too!

[Read down the first letter of each line for a secret message!]

Karma Schmarma

Psychics, ghosts, and tarot cards
Swallowed with a pound of lard

Karma this
Karma that
What a load of Karma scat!

I've seen the rich abuse the poor
Yet stacks of money pile up more
Seen worthless TV 'stars' we know
Make millions off of brand-new shows

It's not true, I tell you this
Hocus Pocus dressed in glitz
If you believe, then you're amiss

And if it's true, what they've all said
May Karma come and strike me dea...

Mmmm Baaacon

I try to sleep
Then hear the peep
No sleep, will I soon reap
May as well just grill those sheep

A tasty rack of lamb!
A succulent spiral ham!
Even a can of seasoned Spam!
I guess that's just what I am!

A non-reflective carnivore
A hearty anti-herbivore
I don't care what may be in store
I'm just a flesh and bone whore

And no, you're not mistaken
My resolve is never shaken
On my death, make sure I'm taken
To a seasoned land of bacon

Some may think it's *Hell*
Me? Just as well
I'd rather consume beast flesh and be flappy
Than consume fibrous bark and be
Crap happy

Shakespeare wrote "Parting is such sweet sorrow." Will
Rogers once said "I've never met a man I didn't like." I never
met either one of them. Coincidence?

AFTERWORD

As a poetry editor I've probably looked at a few thousand books of poetry. Some of it has been very good. After all, what would you expect from a widely acclaimed and well-known poet with a half-dozen bestsellers under his belt? And some of it, frankly, has been pretty amateurish. But once in a while a book will just really jump out at me. *Visions – Adrift in a Sea of Echoes* was such a book.

I'm not really sure why I liked this book so much. Part of it probably has to do with the fact that my dad was a poet. He was really an electrical engineer, but he always said that was only what he did to make a living. Poetry was his first true love. *Visions* reminded me a lot of his work.

One thing I really like about Gary's work is his sly, somewhat dry sense of humor which he occasionally allows us a peek at. This also reminds me a lot of my dad. He could have written some of the poems here, or if not written them he certainly would have appreciated them. It is nice to see a poet who doesn't always take himself so seriously. It's refreshing!

The poetry and prose in the book flows easily, and is straightforward and without pretense. Which is not to say there isn't anything to be said for complex poems with convoluted structures, grammatical tricks, and hidden meanings. There is. Those can be interesting to read and try to figure out. But sometimes I just want a book of poetry I can read for entertainment and enjoyment. I found that here.

Gary handles multiple subjects, and he handles them well. There's a little something for everyone here. In addition, *Visions* is a contribution to the fairly new and still evolving genre of Hybrid Literature. This is a mix of poetry and prose work, and it all must intermesh well and cleanly for it to work. It takes a poet with certain developed skills to do that. Not everybody has that ability, but Gary gives us a primer here on how it's done.

For a debut *Visions* was remarkably good, and I'm confident you will agree with me. I very much look forward to the Hybrid Literature Gary Manz has in store for us in the future!

Don Martin
Tucson, Arizona;
October, 2015

[Don Martin is a best-selling author and editor who lives in Tucson, Arizona. His novels are usually classified as 'high-tech contemporary science fiction,' which he doesn't necessarily agree with, but he takes what he can gets. He also writes the widely-read column *The View From The Streets*, about issues homeless people face. Don is also a music writer and critic (concert and CD reviews, and band interviews) and a book reviewer. When not writing or editing you'll find him reading, mostly politics and history. But not science fiction! He doesn't much enjoy reading what he writes.]

ABOUT THE AUTHOR

Gary Manz is a bright new voice in the world of Hybrid Literature. His insightful poetry has an easy flow and covers topics ranging from general humor to life in general. Readers will especially relate to his outlook on nature, and his unique and often philosophical observations of the world around us. When not writing, you'll often find Gary fishing, reading fiction and the poetry of others, or doing what he loves most other than being next to his wife - driving the countryside and enjoying all its wonders. He lives in the quiet village of Crivitz in the north woods of Wisconsin with his wife Sharon and her sister Susan, and Mekia, their beloved wolf/Shepard mix. Though a poet for over 40 years, he hasn't gone public with his works until recently.

He is featured in the anthology *Beyond The Sea*, released earlier this year, and in the upcoming book *Dad, Me, and the 'OL 66' Pete*, edited by noted children's author Brian Carlson (expected to be released in Nov 2015).